100 Favourite PRAYERS

Compiled by Lois Rock

Illustrated by Sheila Moxley

LION
CHILDREN'S

CONTENTS

Don't worry about anything, but in
your prayers ask God for what you need,
always with a thankful heart.

Based on Philippians 4, in the Bible

My Everyday World

1 Thank you, God in heaven,
For a day begun.
Thank you for the breezes,
Thank you for the sun.
For this time of gladness,
For our work and play,
Thank you, God in heaven,
For another day.

Traditional

A Bright New Day

2 Father, we thank you for the night,
And for the pleasant morning light;
For rest and food and loving care,
And all that makes the day so fair.
Help us to do the things we should,
To be to others kind and good;
In all we do at work or play
To grow more loving every day.

Author unknown

3 This is my prayer number 1:
bless the day that's just begun.

This is my prayer number 2:
may the sky be clear and blue.

This is my prayer number 3:
God, please take good care of me.

This is my prayer number 4:
help me love you more and more.

This is my prayer number 5:
make me glad to be alive.

This is my prayer number 6:
help me when I'm in a fix.

This is my prayer number 7:
make this world a bit like heaven.

This is my prayer number 8:
put an end to hurt and hate.

This is my prayer number 9:
let the light of kindness shine.

This is my prayer number 10:
bring me safe to bed again.

4 This new day is for living,
This new day is for caring,
This new day is for giving,
This new day is for sharing.

5 Dear Lord Jesus, we shall have this day only once; before it is gone, help us to do all the good we can, so that today is not a wasted day.

Stephen Grellet (1773–1855)

6 God be in the little things of all I do today
So at the end the whole may be perfect in every way.

God Cares for Me

7 God, who made the earth,
The air, the sky, the sea,
Who gave the light its birth,
Careth for me.

God, who made the grass,
The flower, the fruit, the tree,
The day and night to pass,
Careth for me.

God, who made all things,
On earth, in air, in sea,
Who changing seasons brings,
Careth for me.

Sarah Betts Rhodes (1824–1904)

8 Help us to remember
All your love and care,
Trust in you and love you,
Always, everywhere.

W. St Hill Bourne (1846–1929)

9 Dear God, you are my shepherd,
You give me all I need,
You take me where the grass grows green
And I can safely feed.

You take me where the water
Is quiet and cool and clear;
And there I rest and know I'm safe
For you are always near.

Based on Psalm 23, in the Bible

10 Jesus, friend of little children,
Be a friend to me;
Take my hand, and ever keep me
Close to thee.

Never leave me, nor forsake me;
Ever be my friend;
For I need thee, from life's dawning
To its end.

Walter J. Mathams (1851–1931)

11 The Lord is
my light and my
salvation;
I will fear no one.
The Lord protects
me from all
danger;
I will never be
afraid.

*From Psalm 27,
in the Bible*

For Those I Love

12 God bless all those that I love;
God bless all those that love me;
God bless all those that love those that I love,
And all those that love those that love me.

From an old sampler

13 Bless the fishes of the sea:
God bless you and God bless me.

Bless the birds that fly above:
God bless everyone I love.

Bless the creatures great and small:
Bless us always, bless us all.

14 God bless the people of this house
In everything they do
And may the love you show to us
be always shining through.

15 Dear God, bless those who visit us: family, friends
and strangers. May we make our home a place of love and
kindness for all. May we share the things we have with
generosity and cheerfulness.

Victoria Tebbs

Out and About

16 May the strength of God pilot us.
May the power of God preserve us.
May the wisdom of God instruct us.
May the hand of God protect us.
May the way of God direct us.
May the shield of God defend us.
May the host of God guard us against the snares
  of evil and the temptations of the world.

St Patrick (389–461)

17 Bless to me, O God,
the work of my hands.
Bless to me, O God,
the work of my mind.
Bless to me, O God,
the work of my heart.

Anonymous

18 Dear God,
When I see someone in trouble,
may I know when to stop and help
and when to hurry to fetch help;
but may I never pass by,
pretending I did not see.

*Prayer based on Jesus' parable of the
Good Samaritan, in the Bible*

19 Father of all mankind, make the roof
of my house wide enough for all opinions,
oil the door of my house so it opens easily
to friend and stranger, and set such a table
in my house that my whole family may
speak kindly and freely around it. Amen.

Prayer from Hawaii

20 O Lord, thou knowest how busy I must be this day.
If I forget thee, do not thou forget me.

Sir Jacob Astley (before the battle of Edgehill, 1642)

Mealtime Graces

21 For health and strength
and daily food,
we praise your name,
O Lord.

Traditional

22 Dear God,
I gratefully bow my head
To thank you for my daily bread,
And may there be a goodly share
On every table everywhere. Amen

A Mennonite children's prayer

23 Here at the table
we join hands in a circle
and remember God's goodness
encircling us all.

24 The bread is warm and fresh,
The water cool and clear.
Lord of all life, be with us,
Lord of all life, be near.

African grace

25 We thank thee, Lord, for happy hearts,
For rain and sunny weather.
We thank thee, Lord, for this our food,
And that we are together.

Emilie Fendall Johnson

26 For food in a world where many walk in hunger;
For faith in a world where many walk in fear;
For friends in a world where many walk alone,
We give you humble thanks, O Lord.

A Girl Guide hunger grace

Faith, Hope, Love

27 To faith, let me add goodness;
to goodness, let me add knowledge;
to knowledge, let me add self-control;
to self-control, let me add endurance;
to endurance, let me add godliness;
to godliness, let me add affection for
   my brothers and sisters;
to affection, let me add love.

From 2 Peter 1:5–7, in the Bible

Faith in God

28 **O**ur God is the God of all,
The God of heaven and earth,
Of the sea and the rivers;
The God of the sun and of the moon and of all the stars;
The God of the lofty mountains and of the lowly valleys,
He has His dwelling around heaven and earth, and sea, and all
    that in them is.

St Patrick (389–461)

29 I believe in God
who made the world
at the very beginning.

I believe in God
who will take care of the world
until its ending.

I believe in God
whose love is for everlasting.

30 I believe,
O Lord and God of the peoples,
that you are
the creator of the high heavens,
that you are
the creator of the skies above,
that you are
the creator of the oceans below.

Carmina Gadelica

31 O God,
as truly as you are our father,
so just as truly you are our mother.
We thank you, God our father,
for your strength and goodness.
We thank you, God our mother,
for the closeness of your caring.
O God, we thank you for the great love
you have for each one of us.

Julian of Norwich (1342–1416)

Saying Prayers

32 I'm sitting
and thinking
and wondering
and wishing
and dreaming
and hoping
and praying

and hoping
and dreaming
and truly
believing
that God
can hear all
that I'm saying.

33 Here I am
    beneath the sky
and all alone
    in prayer;
but I know
    God is listening,
for God is
    everywhere.

34 God the Father,
in heaven above,
hear my prayer
and come close.

God the Son,
in heaven above,
hear my prayer
and come close.

God the Holy Spirit,
in heaven above,
hear my prayer
and come close.

35 O make my heart so still, so still,
When I am deep in prayer,
That I might hear the white mist-wreaths
Losing themselves in air!

Utsonomya San

36 Lord, you know what I want.
If you think it right, may I have it.
If you do not think it right,
good Lord, do not be displeased that I asked,
for I don't want anything that you don't want.

Julian of Norwich (1342–1416)

37 O God,
It is so hard to keep my mind on
my prayers. My thoughts just
run away in a butterfly meadow
of daydreams. Bring me back to
the path that will lead me into
your presence.

Forgiveness

38 I told God everything:
I told God about all the wrong things
   I had done.
I gave up trying to pretend.
I gave up trying to hide.
I knew that the only thing to do was
   to confess.

And God forgave me.

Based on Psalm 32, in the Bible

39 From the mud
a pure white flower

From the storm
a clear blue sky

As we pardon
one another

God forgives us
from on high.

Sophie Piper

40 God, have pity on me, a sinner!

*From Jesus' parable of the Pharisee and
the tax collector, in the Bible*

41 Dear God,
I am not ready to forgive
but I am ready to be made ready.

42 All that we ought to have thought and have not thought,
All that we ought to have said and have not said,
All that we ought to have done and have not done,
All that we ought not to have spoken and yet have spoken,
All that we ought not to have done, and yet have done,
For these words, and works, pray we, O God, for forgiveness.

Traditional

Growing in Wisdom

43 Spirit of God
put love in my life.

Spirit of God
put joy in my life.

Spirit of God
put peace in my life.

Spirit of God
make me patient.

Spirit of God
make me kind.

Spirit of God
make me good.

Spirit of God
give me faithfulness.

Spirit of God
give me humility.

Spirit of God
give me self-control.

From Galatians 5,
in the Bible

44 God be in my head, and in my understanding;
God be in my eyes, and in my looking;
God be in my mouth, and in my speaking;
God be in my heart, and in my thinking;
God be at my end, and at my departing.

Old Sarum primer (1527)

45 O God make me good.
Make me wise.
Make me hardworking.
Make me honest.
Make me tactful.
Make me generous.
Make me truthful.
Make me loyal.
But most of all,
dear God,
make me your child.

Based on Proverbs, in the Bible

46 Lord,
Help me to live this day
Quietly, easily.
Help me to lean upon Thy
Great strength
Trustfully, restfully,
To wait for the unfolding
Of Thy will
Patiently, serenely,
To meet others
Peacefully, joyously,
To face tomorrow
Confidently, courageously.

Amen

*St Francis of Assisi
(1181–1226)*

Obeying the Commandments

47 O Lord,
I have heard your laws.

May I worship you.
May I worship you alone.
May all I say and do show respect for your holy name.
May I honour the weekly day of rest.
May I show respect for my parents.
May I reject violence so that I never take a life.
May I learn to be loyal in friendship and so learn to be faithful in marriage.
May I not steal what belongs to others.
May I not tell lies to destroy another person's reputation.
May I not be envious of what others have, but may I learn to be content
    with the good things you give me.

Based on the Ten Commandments, in the Bible

48 O God,
Your word is a lamp to guide me
and a light for my path.

Psalm 119, in the Bible

Love One Another

49 Help me, Lord, to show your love.

Help me to be patient and kind, not jealous or conceited or proud. May I never be ill-mannered, selfish or irritable; may I be quick to forgive and forget.

May I not gloat over wrongdoing, but rather be glad about things that are good and true.

May I never give up loving: may my faith and hope and patience never come to an end.

Based on 1 Corinthians 13, in the Bible

50 Dear God,
Give us the courage to overcome anger
with love.

51 Dear God,
May I never grow tired of doing good.

From 2 Thessalonians 3, in the Bible

52 Love is giving, not taking,
mending, not breaking,
trusting, believing,
never deceiving,
patiently bearing
and faithfully sharing
each joy, every sorrow,
today and tomorrow.

Anonymous

53 Lord of the loving heart,
May mine be loving too,
Lord of the gentle hands,
May mine be gentle too.
Lord of the willing feet,
May mine be willing too,
So I may grow more like to thee
In all I say and do.

Phyllis Garlick

Following Jesus

54 God, our loving Father, help us remember the birth of Jesus, that we may share in the song of the angels, the gladness of the shepherds and the wisdom of the wise men.

Close the door of hate and open the door of love all over the world.

Let kindness come with every gift and good desires with every greeting.

Deliver us from evil by the blessing which Christ brings and teach us to be merry with clean hearts.

May the Christmas morning make us happy to be your children and the Christmas evening bring us to our beds with grateful thoughts, forgiving and forgiven, for Jesus' sake. Amen.

Robert Louis Stevenson (1850–94)

55 Blessed be the name of Jesus, who died to save us.
Blessed be Jesus, who had compassion on us.
Blessed be Jesus, who suffered loneliness, rejection and
pain, for our sakes.
Blessed be Jesus, through whose cross I am forgiven.
Lord Jesus, deepen my understanding of your suffering
and death.

A prayer from Kenya

56 Thanks be to thee, O Lord Jesus Christ,
for all the benefits which thou hast won for us,
for all the pains and insults which thou hast borne for us.
O most merciful Redeemer, Friend and Brother,
may we know thee more clearly,
love thee more dearly,
and follow thee more nearly,
day by day.

Richard of Chichester (1197–1253)

The Prayer Jesus Taught

57 Our Father in heaven,
hallowed be your name,
your kingdom come,
your will be done,
on earth as in heaven.
Give us today our daily bread.
Forgive us our sins
as we forgive those who sin against us.
Lead us not into temptation
but deliver us from evil.

For the kingdom, the power,
and the glory are yours
now and for ever.
Amen

The traditional Lord's Prayer, based on Matthew 6 and Luke 11, in the Bible

The World We Live In

58 All things bright and beautiful,
All creatures great and small,
All things wise and wonderful,
The Lord God made them all.

Cecil Frances Alexander (1818–95)

The Good Earth

59 All things praise thee Lord most high!
Heaven and earth and sea and sky!

Time and space are praising thee!
All things praise thee; Lord, may we!

George William Condor (1821–74)

60 The sunrise
tells of God's glory;
the moonrise
tells of God's glory;
the starshine
tells of God's glory;
the heavens
tell of God's glory.

*Based on Psalm 19, in
the Bible*

61 For flowers that bloom about our feet,
   Father, we thank Thee,
For tender grass so fresh and sweet, Father,
   we thank Thee,
For the song of bird and hum of bee,
For all things fair we hear or see,
Father in heaven, we thank Thee.

*Ralph Waldo Emerson
(1803–82)*

62 O God, we thank you for this earth,
our home;
for the wide sky and the blessed sun,
for the salt sea and the running water,
for the everlasting hills
and the never-resting winds,
for the trees
and the common grass underfoot.

We thank you for our senses
by which we hear the songs of birds,
and see the splendour of the summer fields,
and taste of the autumn fruits,
and rejoice in the feel of the snow
and smell the breath of the spring.

Grant us a heart
wide open to all this beauty;
and save our souls from being so blind
that we pass unseeing
when even the common thorn bush
is aflame with your glory,
O God our creator,
who lives and reigns for ever and ever.

Walter Rauschenbusch (1861–1918)

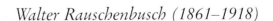

Patterns of the Seasons

63 Thank you, God,
for the unchanging
patterns of the seasons:
the frosts of winter
melting into moist spring,
the rain-soaked buds
unfolding into bright summer,
the flowers fading and falling
in the autumn mist
leaving the year cold and bare,
lit by a pale sun
and the golden promise
of your unfailing love.

64 In winter, God takes a sheet of plain paper
and pencils in the outline of things.

In spring, God brings out a paintbox and washes
the background in blue and green and yellow.

In summer, God adds bright details: pink and red
and orange and mauve.

In the autumn, God scatters golden glitter.

65 God bless the birds of springtime
that twitter in the trees
and flutter in the hedgerows
and soar upon the breeze.

God bless the birds of summer
that gather on the shore
and glide above the ocean
where breakers crash and roar.

God bless the birds of autumn
as they prepare to fly
and fill the damp and chilly air
with wild and haunting cry.

God bless the birds of winter
that hop across the snow
and peck the fallen seeds and fruits
of summer long ago.

66 The sun may shine
the rain may fall
God will always
Love us all.

Victoria Tebbs

Harvest Thanksgiving

67 Dear God,
You are in charge of everything.

You are in charge of the sun and the rain,
the frost and the snow,
the wind and the storm.

You are in charge of the earth and the seed,
the root and the leaf,
the flower and the fruit.

You are in charge of the harvest of the fields
and the harvest of the trees. You give the
world many crops.

And you put us in charge of sharing them.
May we do so in the way that is good and
right and fair.

68 We plough the land,
God sends the rain
to bring the harvest
once again;
and when the fields
of wheat turn gold,
then God's great goodness
must be told.

*Based on Psalm 65,
in the Bible*

69 White are the wavetops,
White is the snow:
Great is the One
Who made all things below.

Green are the grasslands,
Green is the tree:
Great is the One
Who has made you and me.

Blue are the cornflowers,
Blue is the sky:
Great is the One
Who made all things on high.

Gold is the harvest,
Gold is the sun:
God is our Maker –
Great is the One.

70 Thank you, dear God, for our harvest garden.
Thank you for the seeds and the soil,
for the sun and the rain,
for the roots and the leaves and the ripening fruits.
As you have blessed us with harvest gifts, dear God,
may we bless others by sharing them.

All God's Creatures

71 Dear God,
You have made creatures for all the wild and secret places in the world:
for the snowcapped mountain and also the dark ocean floor;
for the rainforest swamp and also the windswept desert;
for each far flung island and also the tiny corners of our gardens:

Teach us, great Maker, to treat the creatures and
their habitats with love and respect.

72 Dear God,
Each tiny creature plays a part in your huge universe.

Please remember each little life and keep that memory safe in your everlasting love.

73 He prayeth best, who loveth best
All things both great and small;
For the dear God who loveth us,
He made and loveth all.

S.T. Coleridge (1772–1834)

74 Bless our little garden. May it be a safe place for all the little creatures that creep and scurry through the grasses. May it be a busy place for all the little creatures that sip and nibble and munch among the flowers. May it be a joyful place for all the birds that sing in the trees.

Our Planet Home

75 God is stronger than all the power in the world:
Even though the wind blows and the trees fall,
even though the rain falls and the rivers flood;
even though the earth shakes and the hillsides crumble
God's love will never end.

Based on Isaiah 53, in the Bible

76 Dear God,
May we walk gently
through this fragile
world.

77 The winter brook flows quick and green
with swirling eddies in between
its tiny falls of sparkling spray
that curl and ripple on their way.

The summer brook is slow and grey
and choked with all we've thrown away:
old cans and bags and battered shoes
and things that we no longer use.

God our Maker, send the rain
to wash the whole world clean again
then teach us to respect and care
for water, fire, earth and air.

78 Save me a clean stream, flowing
to unpolluted seas;

lend me the bare earth, growing
untamed flowers and trees.

May I share safe skies
when I wake, every day,

with birds and butterflies?
Grant me a space where I can play

with water, rocks, trees, and sand;
lend me forests, rivers, hills, and sea.

Keep me a place in this old land,
somewhere to grow, somewhere to be.

Jane Whittle

A Worldwide Family

79 O God,
We are all strangers in this world
and we are all travelling to your country.

So may we not treat anyone as a foreigner
   or an outsider,
but simply as a fellow human being
made in your image.

80 Dear God,
Guard our friendships:

Encourage us,
   that we may encourage one another.

Inspire us,
   that we may inspire one another.

Strengthen us,
   that we may strengthen one another.

Remember us,
   that we may remember one another.

Sophie Piper

81 Dear God,
I am only me and it seems as if the
things I can do are rather small.

Even so, I try to do good things to
make the world a better place.

Please may all the good things I do
be added to all the good things other
people do.

And, dear God, please bless what we
have done so that together we make
a difference.

82 Father God,
Gather us all into a circle of
friendship and circle us about
with your love.

Sophie Piper

Peace on Earth

83 Peaceable Jesus
You took the loaves and fishes
and fed a multitude.

I offer you this day
a tiny gift of squabbles I refused to fight.

Please will you multiply it
among the nations of the world
so that people will turn from war
and live in peace.

Sophie Piper

84 Dear God,
Help me to understand that my
quarrel should not be against other
people, but against quarrelling itself.

Dear God,
Help us all to understand that our
war should not be against other
people, but against war itself.

Mary Joslin

85 God our Father, Creator of the world,
please help us to love one another.
Make nations friendly with other nations;
make all of us love one another like brothers and sisters.
Help us to do our part to bring peace in the world
and happiness to all people.

Prayer from Japan

86 O God, make us
children of quietness
and heirs of peace.

St Clement (1st century)

87 Lord, make me an instrument of your peace.
Where there is hatred, let me sow love;
Where there is injury, pardon;
Where there is discord, union;
Where there is doubt, faith;
Where there is despair, hope;
Where there is darkness, light;
Where there is sadness, joy.

O divine Master, grant that I may not so much
seek to be consoled as to console, to be understood
as to understand, to be loved as to love; for it is in
giving that we receive, it is in pardoning that we are
pardoned, and it is in dying that we are born to
eternal life.

Attributed to St Francis of Assisi (1181–1126)

God Bless Us All

88 May the Lord bless you,
may the Lord take care of you;
May the Lord be kind to you,
may the Lord be gracious to you;
May the Lord look on you with favour,
may the Lord give you peace.

Based on Numbers 6, in the Bible

God Comforts Us

89 O God,
You have not made us for darkness
but for light.

You have not made us for sorrow
but for joy.

You have not made us for death
but for life.

So lead us all into your presence.

90 We pray for those for whom today
is like the windswept mountain:
give them comfort.

We pray for those for whom today
is like the stormy sea:
give them calm.

We pray for those for whom today
is like the darkest night:
give them hope.

Sophie Piper

91 Every day
in silence we remember
those whom we loved
to whom we have said a last goodbye.
Every day
in silence we remember.

92 O God,
be to me
like the evergreen tree
and shelter me in your shade,
and bless me again
like the warm gentle rain
that gives life to all you have made.

Based on Hosea 14, in the Bible

Night-time Prayers

93 Thank you, God in heaven, for the blue sky of the morning.
Thank you, God in heaven, for the golden sun of day.
Thank you, God in heaven, for the shadows of the evening.
Thank you, God, for watching me all through the busy day.

94 Now I lay me down to sleep,
I pray thee, Lord, thy child to keep;
Thy love to guard me through the night
And wake me in the morning light.

Traditional

95 The moon shines bright,
The stars give light
Before the break of day;
God bless you all
Both great and small
And send a joyful day.

Traditional

96 Lord, keep us safe this night,
Secure from all our fears;
May angels guard us while we sleep,
Till morning light appears.

John Leland (1754–1841)

Partings and Blessings

97 **M**ay the road rise to meet you.
May the wind be always at your back.
May the sun shine warm upon your face,
the rains fall soft upon your fields and,
until we meet again,
may God hold you in the palm of his hand.

Irish blessing

98 **M**ay the Lord Jesus
be your light in the darkness;
your warmth in the cold;
your happiness in sorrow.

99 Peace of the running waves to you,
Deep peace of the flowing air to you,
Deep peace of the quiet earth to you,
Deep peace of the shining stars to you,
Deep peace of the shades of night to you,
Moon and stars always giving light to you,
Deep peace of Christ, the Son of Peace, to you.

Traditional Gaelic blessing

100 Wherever you go,
May God the Father be with you.
Wherever you go,
May God the Son be with you.
Wherever you go,
May God the Spirit be with you.

Index of first lines